ULTIMATE
BUILDING IDEAS

Ultimate Building Ideas

Copyright © 2019

All rights reserved. No portion of the book may be reproduced or utilized in any form or by any means electronic or mechanical, including photocopying, recording or by any other informational storage and retrieval system.

Table of Contents

Introduction **6**
Emerald Farming **7**
Storage Rooms **8**
Sandstone Mansion **9**
Pyramids **10**
Graveyard **11**
Hotels **12**
Robots **13**
3D Models **14**
Museum **15**
Town Hall **16**
Navy Destroyer **17**
Death Star **18**
Bridge **19**
Cities **20**
Volcano **21**
Barn **22**

Harbour 23
Theme Park 24
Mountains 25
Ski Resort 26
Hockey Arena 27
Basketball Court 28
Colosseum 29
The Globe Theatre 30
Water Features 31
Ancient Ruins 32
Jail 33
Tanks 34
Pirate Ship 35
Military Barracks 36
Yacht 37
Spaceships 38
Pixel Art 39
Helicopter 40
Eiffel Tower 41

Ultimate Building Ideas

McDonald's 42
Bank 43
Submarine 44
Small Race Car 45
2x2 Redstone Door 52
Water Elevator 60
Obsidian Generator: 65
Jail: 74
Redstone Flip Switch 82
Auto-Smelting 88
Sphere 93
Truck 100
Conclusion 108

~ 5 ~

Introduction

Minecraft is one of the most popular video games in the world, and one of the main reasons for this is the ability for just about anyone to jump into the game, and build anything they can dream of. There really is no limit to what you can create, only your imagination is holding you back!

But that doesn't mean that it's not a good idea to get some helpful tips from others along the way. Minecraft has been around for a long time now, and there are some very experienced builders out there. So in this guide, we hope we can provide you with the basic skills and ideas you can use to create something amazing and original in the world of Minecraftia!

Emerald Farming

Emerald Farming is a great way to obtain valuable items. Trading with Villagers to obtain emeralds is known as Emerald Farming. Here is an example of an Emerald Farm.

Storage Rooms

For people with lots of items, a larger storage room is needed. Using Trapped Chests, a wall of chests can be created. Add an item frame with an item that represents what each chest contains to complete to room!

Ultimate Building Ideas

Sandstone Mansion

Smooth Sandstone is a great material to use in building mansions. It goes great with diamonds and quartz, as well as stone brick.

Ultimate Building Ideas

Pyramids

Pyramids are fun to build because of their simplistic design and versatility. Pyramids can be made out of any block! Decorate the inside however you like. You could create a maze, storage room, house, or whatever else you could think of!

Ultimate Building Ideas

Graveyard

Visit the souls of those lost in Minecraft. Build a memorial to your fallen friends!

Ultimate Building Ideas

Hotels

Need a place to sleep? No problem! Charge your friends a diamond every time they sleep in this beautiful hotel

Ultimate Building Ideas

Robots

Gigantic robots are always a welcomed sight!

Ultimate Building Ideas

3D Models

Have somebody you want to build? It can be done!

Ultimate Building Ideas

Museum

Have something you want to show off? Did you finally get a Wither Skull? Put it in a museum! Use item frames to hold items!

Town Hall

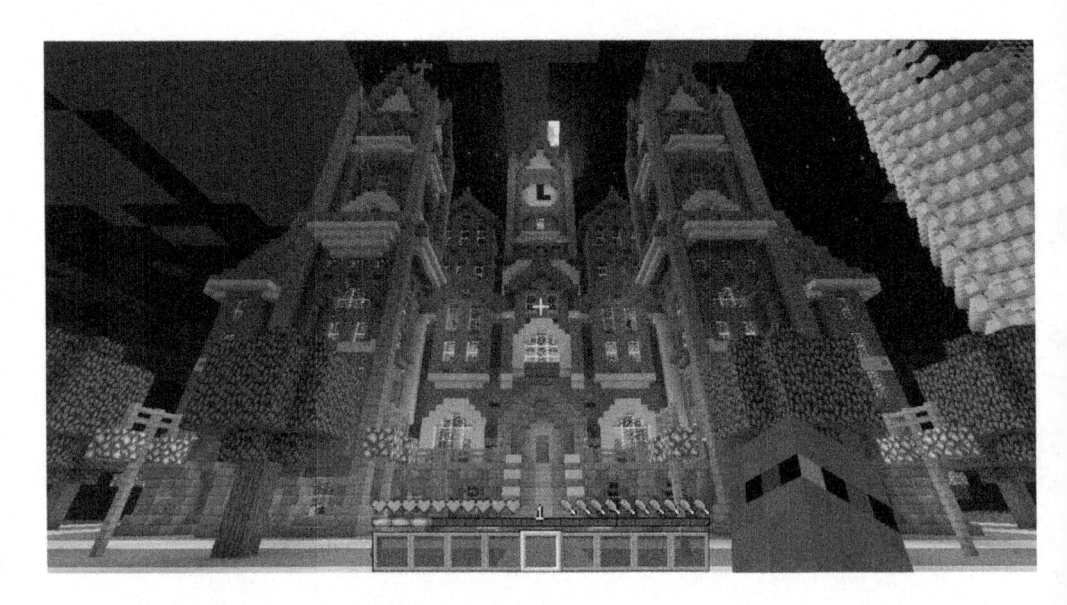

Perfect place for all the villagers to discuss what they are going to be trading next!

Ultimate Building Ideas

Navy Destroyer

A large Navy Vessel in Minecraft is always a great build!

~ 17 ~

Ultimate Building Ideas

Death Star

It might be broken, but it's definitely not forgotten!

Ultimate Building Ideas

Bridge

Cross that pool of lava in style!

Ultimate Building Ideas

Cities

Build up your very own metropolis!

Ultimate Building Ideas

Volcano

Watch out for that lava!

Ultimate Building Ideas

Barn

Make a nice home for your animals!

Harbour

A safe place to unload all the precious cargo from your mining adventures!

Ultimate Building Ideas

Theme Park

Even Villagers need to have some fun once in a while

Mountains

Scale the icy slope and make it to the peak of the gigantic mountain!

Ski Resort

If climbing mountains isn't your cup of tea, then you should relax at a ski lodge!

Ultimate Building Ideas

Hockey Arena

Challenge your friends to an ice-cold game of hockey!

Ultimate Building Ideas

Basketball Court

Can that Villager even dunk?

Ultimate Building Ideas

Colosseum

Travel back in time and fight gladiators!

Ultimate Building Ideas

The Globe Theatre

If gladiators scare you, perhaps watching a Shakespearean play would be more appealing!

Water Features

Add some flare to your build by adding Water Features! A fountain, pool, or even a bathtub are all great ways to incorporate water into your design.

Ultimate Building Ideas

Ancient Ruins

Deep in the jungle you find yourself a ruined temple! Use lots of cracked and mossy stone to build this haunting creation

Ultimate Building Ideas

Jail

That Villager is up to no good! Throw him in the slammer!

Ultimate Building Ideas

Tanks

Got creeper problems? Blow them away with your very own fleet of heavy duty tanks!

Pirate Ship

Sail off into the land of blocks and creepers in an amazing Pirate Ship. Use wool for the masts, and create an awesome poop-deck!

e Building Ideas

Military Barracks

Now your army of villagers will have a comfortable place to rest before battling hordes of creepers.

Ultimate Building Ideas

Yacht

Live a life of luxury in a super-large yacht!

Spaceships

In Minecraft, spaceships can be very complex!

Pixel Art

Using coloured wool, Pixel Art can be created! Almost anything can be created with pixel art, from video game characters to flowers to cars!

Helicopter

Escape the wrath of the Wither in a Helicopter!

Eiffel Tower

Take a trip to Paris without leaving your living room!

Ultimate Building Ideas

McDonald's

Hungry? Why not build your very own fast food joint?!

Bank

Need to make a deposit? Make sure the creeper doesn't blow up the vault!

Ultimate Building Ideas

Submarine

Do some deep-sea diving in this amazing vessel!

Ultimate Building Ideas

Small Race Car

Step 1:

Make a 7x3 frame with Black Wool

Ultimate Building Ideas

Step 2:

Fill in with stone slabs

Ultimate Building Ideas

Step 3:

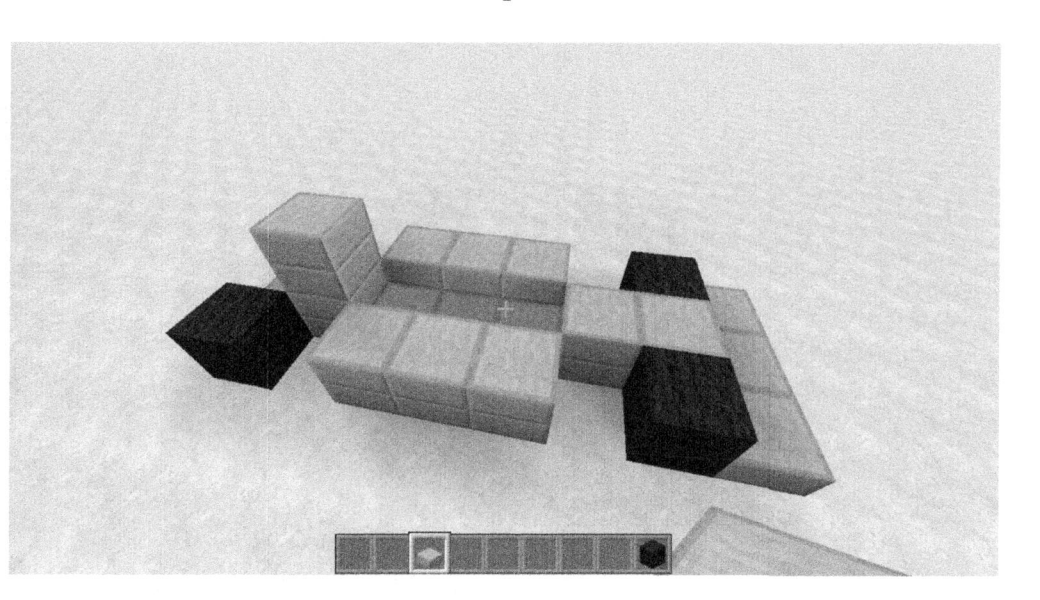

Place stone slabs on top

Ultimate Building Ideas

Step 4:

Raise the back stone slab up to 3

Ultimate Building Ideas

Step 5:

Using 3 stone slabs, make a spoiler

Ultimate Building Ideas

Step 6:

Dig one block down and replace it with a stone slab. Put a rail on top of that.

Ultimate Building Ideas

Step 2:

Make a 2 tall tower 1 block behind the sticky pistons, and place a redstone torch on the side. This will activate the pistons

Ultimate Building Ideas

Step 3:

Make a redstone wire down...

Into the ground, on both sides

Step 4:

Make a 2x3 redstone rectangle underneath the surface

Ultimate Building Ideas

Step 5:

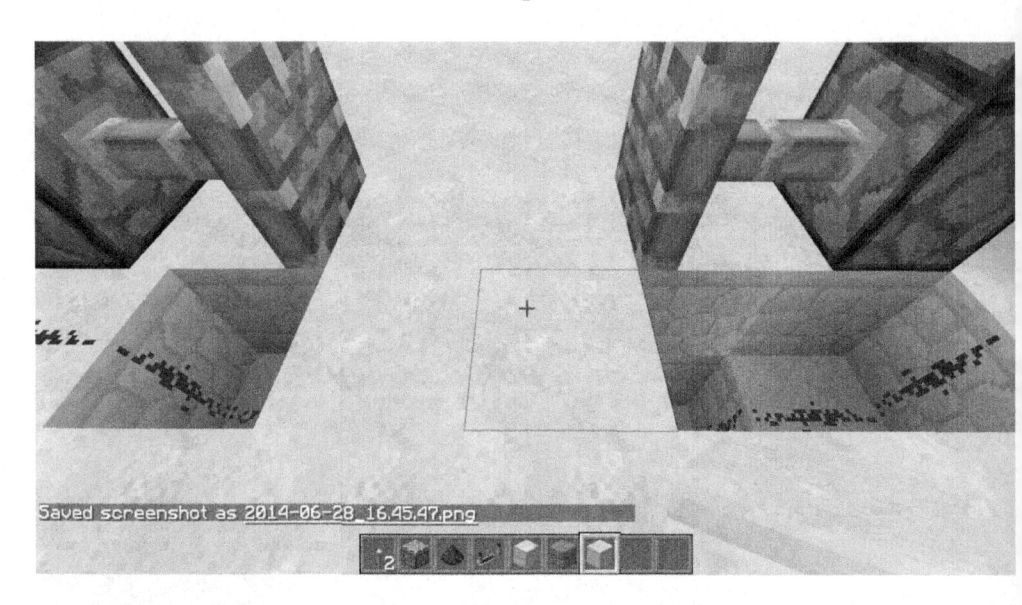

Cover it up

Step 6:

Place pressure plates on the 2 blocks before and after the pistons

Ultimate Building Ideas

Step 7:

Place the blocks that will be the "door"

Ultimate Building Ideas

Step 8:

Seal and enjoy!

Water Elevator

Step 1:

Create a tower like this, any height

Ultimate Building Ideas

Step 2:

Create a 2-tall opening at the bottom

Ultimate Building Ideas

Step 3:

Place signs every other block, starting from the 2nd block

Ultimate Building Ideas

Step 4:

Repeat Step 3 with water, placing it between the signs

Ultimate Building Ideas

Step 5:

Now walk into the bottom and hold {SPACE} to move up! Enjoy!

Ultimate Building Ideas

Obsidian Generator:

Step 1:

Dig a 5x4 hole, 2 blocks down

Ultimate Building Ideas

Step 2:

Dig one more block down on the sides

Ultimate Building Ideas

Step 3:

Dig 1 block into the wall

Ultimate Building Ideas

Step 4:

Add water to each block in this "shelf"

Ultimate Building Ideas

Step 5:

Place redstone

Step 6:

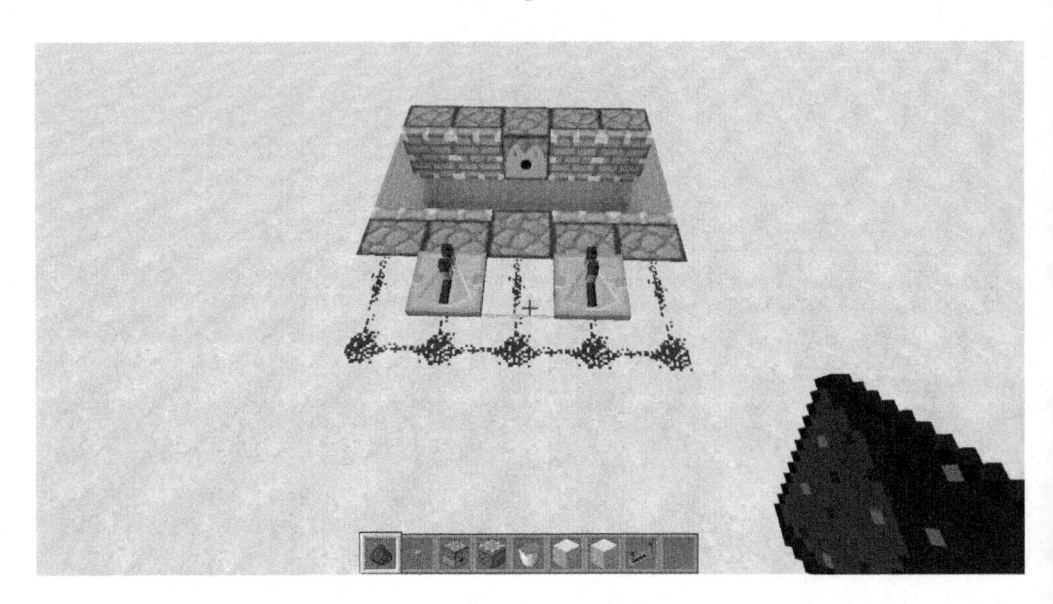

Using redstone, repeaters, pistons and dispensers, arrange the outside like this:

Step 7:

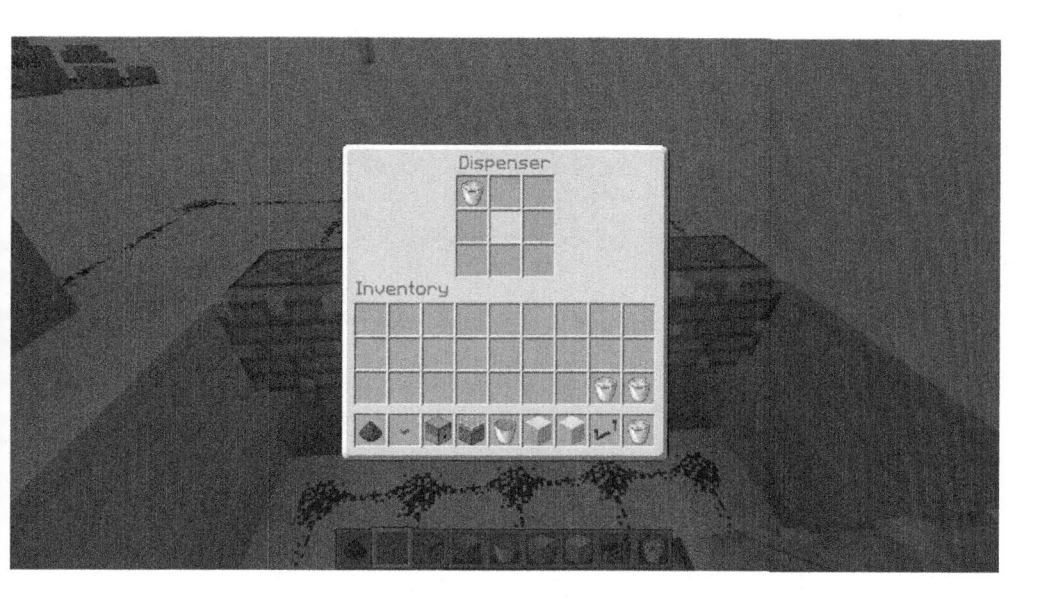

Put lava into the dispensers

Ultimate Building Ideas

Step 8:

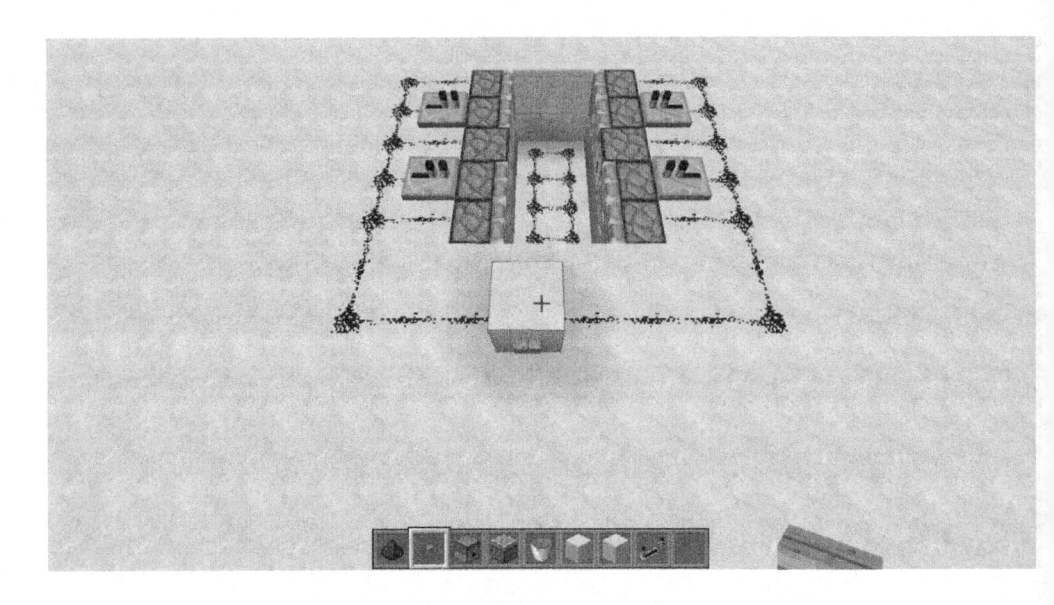

Connect the redstone circuit and add a button

Step 9:

Press the button and wait for the lava to cover all the redstone, then press it again. You will see that there is a nice sheet of obsidian to mine!

Ultimate Building Ideas

Jail:

Step 1:

Create a square or rectangle of stone brick. This can be any size.

Ultimate Building Ideas

Step 2:

Add stairs wherever you like

Ultimate Building Ideas

Step 3:

Make a doorway, and put up walls around the floor

Ultimate Building Ideas

Step 4:

Add furnishings for the prisoner, and make 2 windows out of iron fence

Ultimate Building Ideas

Step 5:

Add the jail cell bars using iron fence

Ultimate Building Ideas

Step 6:

Make a roof

Ultimate Building Ideas

Step 7:

Add Iron Doors, for extra protection

Step 8:

Enjoy your life with this prisoner locked up!

Redstone Flip Switch

This small contraption will allow buttons and pressure plates to work like levers

Step 1:

Place 2 sticky pistons 4 blocks apart

Step 2:

In front of one of the pistons, dig 1 block down and place a redstone torch

Ultimate Building Ideas

Step 3:

Place a block on top of the torch, and then 2 blocks above

Step 4:

Put redstone torches on each end, above the pistons

Ultimate Building Ideas

Step 5:

Place redstone on the 2 blocks, then bring it 1 block down. Add a button

Step 6:

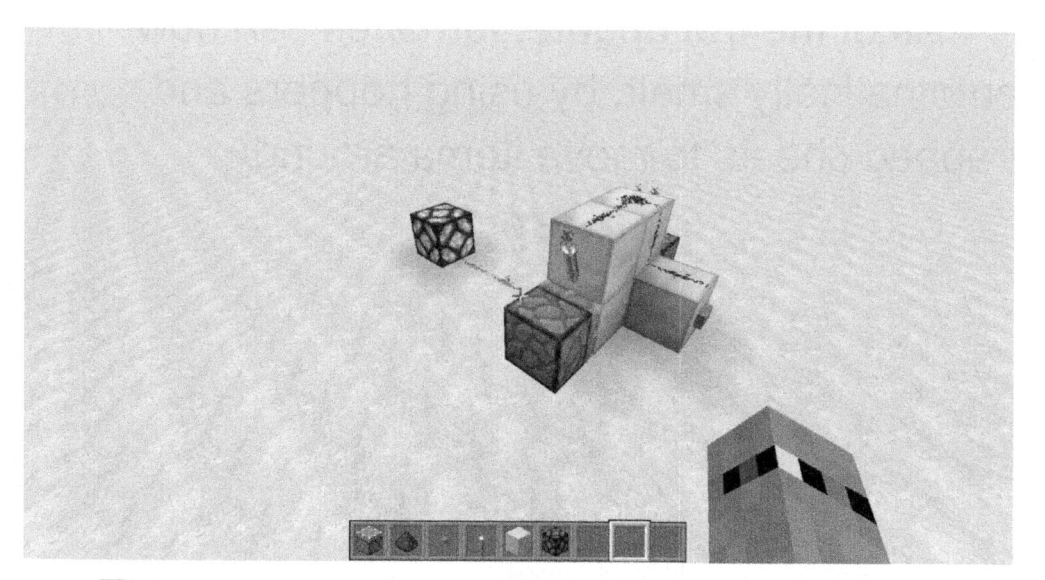

This can now be used to power whatever redstone device you need, just make a redstone circuit off the end

Ultimate Building Ideas

Auto-Smelting

As of the 1.6 update, furnaces can now automatically smelt, by using hoppers and trapped chests to move items around

Step 1:

Place a chest, The hopper attached (hold shift and right click the chest while holding the hopper to attach). Place a furnace above the hopper

Ultimate Building Ideas

Step 2:

Attach a hopper to the side of the furnace, and another one above

Ultimate Building Ideas

Step 3:

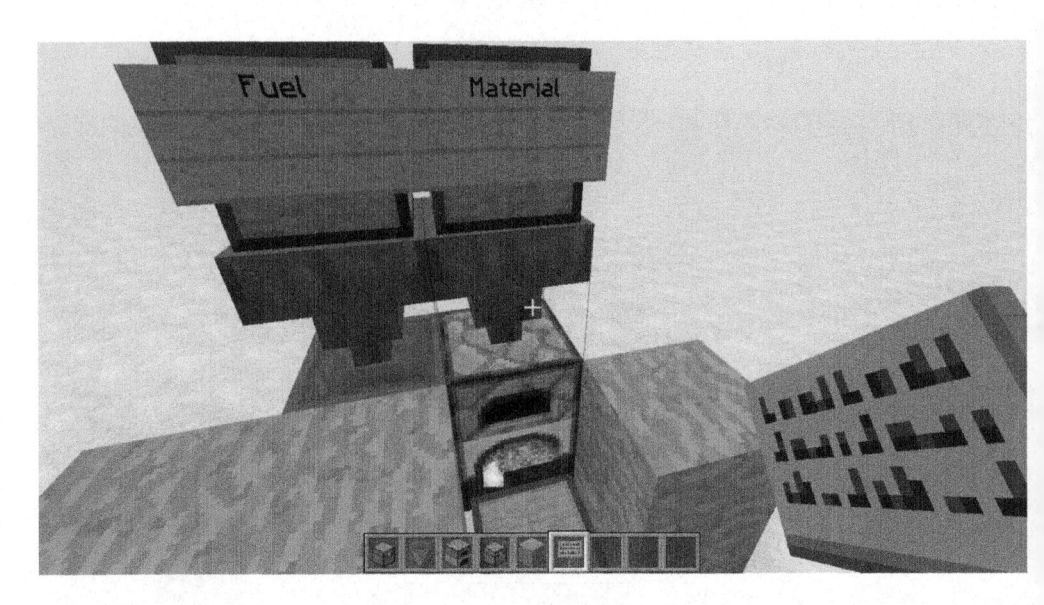

Place a chest above one of the hoppers, and a trapped chest above the other. Label the chest directly above the furnace as "Material" and the other as "Fuel"

Step 4:

Now when you place your items in the respective chest, the furnace will automatically start to smelt

Ultimate Building Ideas

Step 5:

The products will be found in the chest on the ground!

Sphere

Spheres are very complex shapes that can be made in Minecraft. It takes some time, but hard work always pays off.

Step 1:

Create a 1x7 tower 1 block off the ground

Ultimate Building Ideas

Step 2:

From the middle block, extend 3 blocks outward in all directions

Step 3:

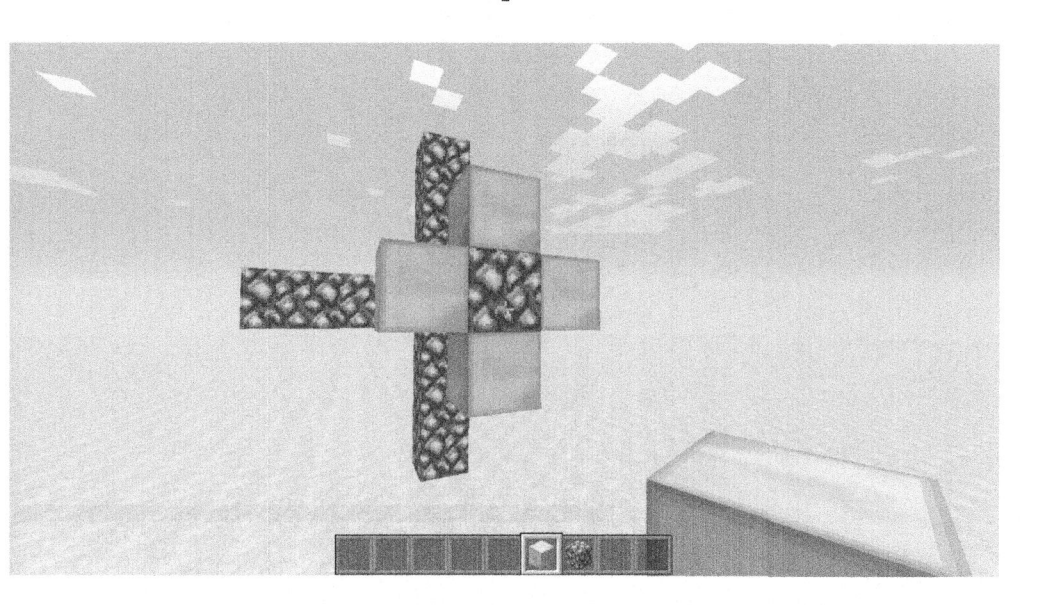

At the end of each shaft, put your block of choice around the edges.

Step 4:

Do this for each shaft

Step 5:

For the 4 shafts coming out from the middle, follow this pattern. Basically, make a square behind the end of the shaft and break off the corners.

Step 6:

When all middle shafts have been completed, you should be left with 4 holes on the top. Fill them in.

Ultimate Building Ideas

Step 6:

Do the same for the bottom, and you will have a perfect sphere!

Ultimate Building Ideas

Truck
Step 1

Place black wool in the following pattern. It can be adjusted to fit the size you want.

Ultimate Building Ideas

Step 2

Fill the front in with stone slabs

Ultimate Building Ideas

Step 3:

Construct the cabin

Step 4:

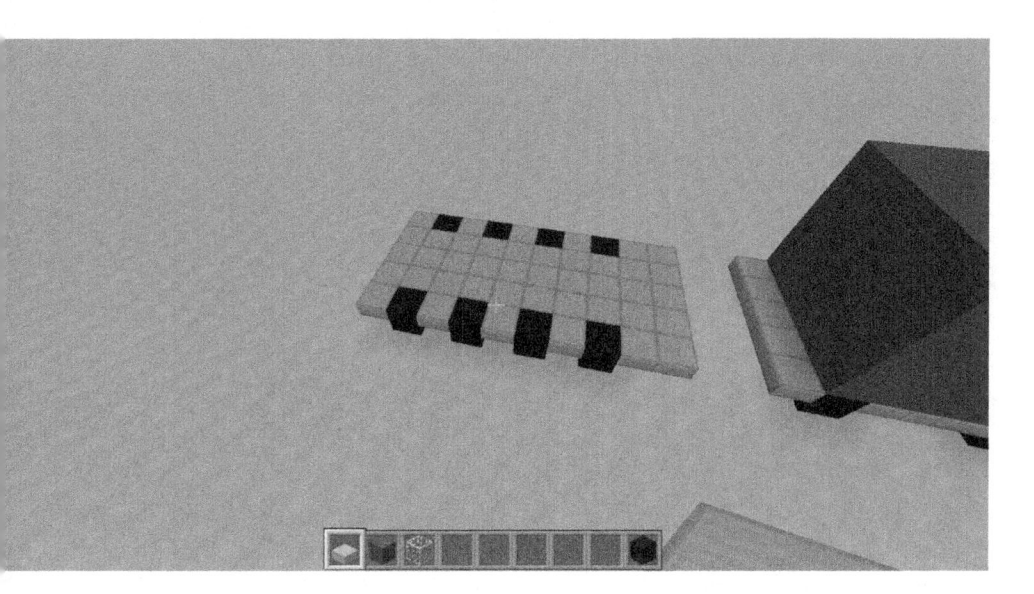

Fill in the trailer with stone slabs

Ultimate Building Ideas

Step 5:

Create the hitch between trailer and cabin

Step 6:

Build up the trailer.

Step 7:

Add the exhaust. Cobwebs can be used to look like smoke!

Step 8:

Add some details and you are good to go!

Conclusion

This guide has provided you with some insight and inspiration to begin your Minecraft projects. These examples should help server as an example of what can be accomplished with a little imagination, and a lot of heart.

Made in the USA
Monee, IL
28 March 2021